Notes From the Field

Sasha Wade

RED MARE
PRESS

NOTES FROM THE FIELD

Edited by Elyssia Nguyen and Sara Dudo.

Cover design by Emelie Mano.

Interior design by Julianne Johnson.

Red Mare Press / Discover New Art, LLC
70 SW Century Drive, Suite 100442, Bend, Oregon 97702

www.redmarepress.com

Red Mare Press is a division of Discover New Art, LLC.
The Red Mare Press name and logo are trademarks of
Discover New Art, LLC.
The publisher is not responsible for websites (or their content) that are not owned by the publisher.

ISBN 979-8-9939024-4-9

Printed in the United States of America.

CONTENTS

White Buck

Among the herd, your soft-target swagger
disturbs evening light. *Come look,* I beg

my husband who calls the buck—bleached
by leucism—ugly. I see a creature rarer

than beauty, a double-horned deer floating
uninterrupted between evergreen branches

lowered by snow. He glides as if myth
resides deep in his flesh, informing his

smooth, traceable tracks: like an ordinary
moon casting its shadow on earth to block

sunlight. We are an uncommon phenomenon
of alignment, Stag. It hurts to take my eyes

off you: not because I care what you may
stand for—purification, singularity, the after-

world—Christ. I, too, know how to be
whatever a lover, hunter, mother, child wants

me to be—the art of hide easily mastered.
But how do you roam so free from the weight

of human projections, desires? Let me rake
my fingers through the washed-out white

of your buckskin, brush the back of my hand
along your uneven spine where the secret

to your certainty, peace lies. To be inside
the fullness of creature, look up unstartled by

the hawk's circling, or stranger's stare. No.
I'm lying. All I want is your weightlessness

in cold air: to feel sorrow carried off by
wind, a sorrow the color of winter's heather.

How I Lost You in Winter

Limbless, floating bubble
listen to your heart beat
your eyes like barren craters
as if struck by omniscience
When the click of sonogram keys
circling my womb for sonic
or, are you as big as
hide-and-seek with Hera
across the skies, creating
Hands interlocked, I cradle
to enter the room soon, to tell
Yes, I lack a proper sac
to nurse you. Rusty, scarred
the truth: in a younger mother's
tissue, you would have
forgive myself, her.
premature buds. Plastic
wonder if you've lived
my thoughts as your own, if
not giving you lungs to last
falling. Before they say
for good, let's orbit out
in slow-spin—collapsing
earth's atmosphere. Far,
an ordinary squall tearing
unearthing the farmer's lot.
see field-stones blink like

you are corded still. I
wobble and fade, watch
on a buzzing screen, stare back
or can we call it love?
freeze, I fear the lunar wand
heat has lost you
a boy's thumb, playing
who sprayed her breast milk
star clots. The Milky Way.
my neck, expecting the doctor
me my bleeding is a blessing.
packed with oxygen-rich cells
uterus of mine, I hate
womb stuffed with fertile
thrived. For this, I can barely
The willow trees lack grace,
blinds block white sky, while I
long enough to hear
so, forgive me. Forgive me for
black eyelashes to catch snow
your pulse has stopped
of this hospital bed
heart of ours—beyond
far, but close enough to see
up the once-blue lake,
So much dust. Look. Can you
dulled stars half-buried in dirt?

Mummy Child

After The Mummy Child Exhibit: Museum of Fine Arts, Houston

I long for the scrape of your crawl
down the hallway
where I'll teach you about shadows—

how tiny finger claws can make
a swan's beak on a blank wall. I long

to unravel you, free your resin-
layered flesh from
a thousand-year exile, slip my hand

through your raised rib cage to touch
the bloodless indent of almost feeling.

If I rock you in a wooden cradle, rattle
your chest to check
for a distant pulse, swaddle your bones

in blankets until your veins fill up, will
soft black lashes blink, again? Forgive

me, my intentions, as I pump your limbs
back into the perpetual shape
of a child. Teach me, child, the sting

of oxygen softening marbled lungs,
the smell of cries stumbling. Make me

believe, when early spring infects snow
with steady ice-taps of rain,
my children, too, will live forever.

What Van Gogh Knew

After his painting "The Good Samaritan"

We stay with the painting, my daughter and I,
for such a long time, seduced by three forms
caught in slow motion on a dirt-dusted road
cut between mountains. *This is not the story
of a Good Samaritan,* my daughter says to
me. I see how the samaritan struggles to lift
the dying man onto the donkey's motionless
back. Perhaps the animal smelled the blood
of the beaten man first, heard his groans, and
refused to go on without him. His master,
though kind, had no choice. A priest cloaked
in black—his back turned to the donkey, the two
men, the lifting—never stopped. *He is without
animal. This is the real story,* my daughter
whispers. Her hands move us forward, closer
into the scene, as her eyes confirm what she
believed Van Gogh knew: God wanted us to
see the world just like this: frozen in jagged
sweeps of color—burnt yellows lifted by
blue—the entire human race caught in light.

Mummy Child Meditates

After The Mummy Child Exhibit: Museum of Fine Arts, Houston

Listen: it makes me shudder,
your obsession with me—
my stained gauze-skin,
my hollowed-out rowboat

of a body—what are you
after? Yes, my blue-hearted
lungs were pulled from my
chest, reinserted for endurance.

You stare like you want to
caress the compressed stump
of my childhood. You want
too much. Go listen for the ache

of a bird song too far away
to follow, caught in winds
rearranging the river. Imagine
the last few seconds never

happening. Imagine the unrest
of forever with no music.
If that's why you're here,
find the child who visits

me every week and every
week she asks her mother,
*Is there really a little girl
underneath all that wrapping?*

Yes, the mother says to her.
Don't you want to know
what the girl says to me
every week? Go find her.

Where My Mother Goes

Even though we are in our sixties, we do what sisters do—talk about the past, compare childhood notes, compete. My sisters say, of the three of us, I am the closest to our mother—who, they now claim, was never easy to be close to. Unlike my father, who was always hugging us, my mother showed her love from a distance. A child learned to read her like a still-life painting that changes with light. When I was four, my grandmother died at fifty-nine years old. Our mother grew quiet. Every morning after my father and older siblings left for school, my mother and I walked to St. Agnes Church to light a candle. Kneeling in front of the Virgin Mother, I repeated "Hail Mary," the only prayer I knew, over and over to myself. On our way home, we crossed Grand Army Plaza in Prospect Park, where I loved to stare up at the statues of two bronze horses with winged angels by their side. A tall woman, waving a sword in the air, stood between them, but she was so far away, I couldn't see her face. Together, the statues looked as if they were marching across the sky. When we crossed the park to go home to Montgomery Place, I counted the numbers on each brownstone until I read thirty-two. We lived on the first floor and The Dwyer family lived on the top two floors. Sometimes we played outside with their children, but we hardly ever saw Mrs. Dwyer. My mother said Mrs. Dwyer was too young to have so many children. Each day after lunch, my mother would go into her bedroom, pull down the shades, get into bed, and close her eyes. I followed her in, knowing she would have a box of crayons and white paper on her bedside table. I learned to draw on the floor next to the window where slits of daylight peeked through. While I was alone in the room with my mother, I learned that her love for her mother was so enormous, part of her heart had to rest in order to travel where my grandmother had gone. I learned silence, too, and what a room feels like when something is broken but never falls. Sometimes, when my mother was asleep, I played with a special doll she kept in her bottom bureau drawer next to a pile of rosary beads wrapped in tissue paper. The doll wore a red dress, and her long arms were raised half-way up in the air as if she was dancing a wild dance and something stopped her. I liked to pretend the doll had invisible horses and angels to carry her away, just like the statue of the woman in the park. I didn't tell my sisters about the doll because I didn't want to share it, or maybe I didn't want them to know Mum slept all afternoon. It was a secret, like when someone dies and no one talks about what happened.

Elegy For Paul Monette: *1945-1995*

October 1976: The long New England light
climbed to our third-floor classroom
where we'd arrive early, waiting for you
to turn the corner, wearing a scarf
you never took off during class—often tan
or clay-colored—twined to keep your throat
warm, steady. Like your voice, which was always
seconds ahead of your rarely blinking eyes
lashed long and brown as a deer.
       I fell in love with you. The idea of you.
Both. Something about your chin-raise
as you prodded the nothingness of silence
until even our breath ceased in advance
of your words: *Listen, as I read. What is the heart
of the poem?* At seventeen, what did I know
of truth, the heart, the poem "Falling"
by James Dickey about a real-life stewardess
sucked out of a plane's cracked door.
          Imagine the impact
as we listened, open-mouthed, to her spiraling
through the atmosphere—clawing
at airlessness—desperate to scream. I, too,
began to see her transform: a goddess-bird coasting
with winged arms, her long-range owl
eyes scanning for water, or a soft loam to land
        in. The October sunlight
burned yellow to white, as the rotational roar
of voices—hers, the poets, yours—careened
    into one thrum of ecstatic terror.

What does the poet imagine, you asked us,
the stewardess struggles to do before she lands,
tragically, back-first in a Kansas wheat field?
       Though the poem was not the truth
of her descent, I'll never forget what I imagined
that day—not just her falling—but how she might
have tried to live knowing she'd never survive.
       And I never imagined
after you left the east coast, found and lost love,
how soon you'd battle for more time to outpace
cells, to voice your grief, rage. Decades later, watching
the documentary of your life, I see you at the end,
skeletal in a hotel room in DC, hooked up to IVs
for hours, hoping to march against hate, bigotry.
       Did you know then
how much, like faded lines on the white marble
blocks in Greece, the written remains
of your life would speak into the future? Now,
reading your elegy "Here" for Rog, is hearing
your voice again: like farewell light shaking, tumbling
through immortal space, sirening back
                the little thing of telling the hill—
the same green hill at Forest Lawn where you are
buried now—*Oh, I'm here, I'm here.*

Ecstasy of Quiet Birds

I stake stems of not-yet-bloomed peonies
into a vase. This before-bloom of buds, urgent

and tight, is an ache I miss. Exquisite, how pooled
in water, they pause to hold their breath. I want

to trust this *single house* species, where male
and female structures work as one in the same

flower; as if being self-sufficient, seemingly
complete, can sustain. Brushing sepal-smudge

off my fingers feels final, like the last touch
of a departing lover's shirtsleeve, wrist-skin—

yours. Our ending. So unlike how we began.
Two hawks extending wings wide across skies,

destination undisclosed. Was it courage, or hubris
that made us want to fly. I'm older now. Reality—

call it despair—grounds me in non-flight where
the earth demands endpoints, surrender. Standing

in my kitchen alone, staring at beauty, I'm stuck
on the inevitable sloughing of things. Look! Here

comes the expected parade: garish whites, pinks,
bursting open. Soon, sudden peonies, splayed

on top of green stalks, swirling parasols, their lurid
preening mirrored in glass tabletops. Only days later,

outer guard petals will loosen, drop. Next, inner
corollas fall fast, faster, followed by a dark scattering

of pollen-beads that leave stamen, pistil—drained—
exposed. What a show, for an ecstasy so brief.

I can't stand to look at them. These perennials,
with their vital crowns, overreaching root system,

thriving under-ground in winter's live rot. Such
awful renewal, cycling in and out of strangers' lives,

losses, shamelessly on display. They mock me, year
after year. My finite body. The unobserved birds.

Our Geography

For my great grandfather, Alirio Diaz Guerra

Strangers. Our hands never touched, yet my fingers
    flip piles of parched pages on microfiche
        searching for some pulse, a sign your words

migrated—mumbled over miles—waiting to be
    found. I am your little poem-stalker, lost
        in a language my mother never spoke,

a language you loved. Where are the traces of you
    in me? Not even a color-match in the only
        photograph you left us—retina-clouded

eyes fixed blue behind thick glasses. Can oceans shift
    continents closer together over time? Once
        a stranger in your homeland, Colombia, I

searched for you at the Cathedral Basilica in Bogota.
    Pressing my hands on the back of the pew
        where you rested yours 100 years ago, I

rolled my palms into polished wood and waited for
    a jolt of blood-echoes. Tell me how it felt
        to be exiled from Bogota to New York,

"to nail down your desolate tent in another light,"
    in Brooklyn—the place where I was born.
        Does the heart forever miss home? I

returned to walk from St. Agnes Church to Prospect
      Park, ground marked by your footsteps, then
            mine, decades between us. Paper-thin

cherry blossom crushed on cobblestone—children
      running to grass. Soles, blossoms, cells, our silt
            cemented. Milagro. Here, in this island-city

anchored by bridges, where you wrote about the myth
      of the American Dream. Here, where I roam with,
            without you. Your shadow, behind, beside me.

Santa Maria La Blanca

I dreamed day-light dragged
behind the iron-rusted train.
A girl, eyes silver-salted,
stretched her legs beyond

an open boxcar, feet almost
touching fields of yellow
rapeseed flying by. Half-awake,
I watched night turn dawn

into rivers of peach sand. I
heard ancient desert air
singe the girl's throat, twisting
her long, damp hair into

knotted dust-clouds circling
the clay city of vacant domes—
Toledo. Having never left,
her voice returned to rise out

of the scalloped windows
of Santa Maria La Blanca.
Shuddering in heat, rain seeped
through the girl's teeth. A rain

of a thousand lost names—
slaughtered—gushed from her
throat, crushing crosses
and pillars, flooding streets

with invisible footsteps,
drowning the western ghetto
with syllables unspoken since
1401, when the Dominicans

came to rename the Synagogue
"St. Mary in White," converting
the mosque to a chapel
of alabaster. Its horse-shoe arcs

are bleached, chalked by erasure.
Outside the church's white-
washed walls, people pray for
ancestors who rolled up their

tongues, refused the host. Prayers
to remember them, not as
apparitions greyish blue, but as
the names the girl sang all night.

NOTES

"Elegy For Paul Monette: 1945-1995" includes reference to "Falling" by James Dickey and is written after Paul Monette's poem "Here" in *Love Alone: Eighteen Elegies for Rog.*

"Our Geography" is written after Alirio Diaz Guerra's poem "Voces Íntimas" (Intimate Voices).

ACKNOWLEDGMENTS

Rust & Moth: "Mummy Child," "Mummy Child Meditates"

Winner of the 2023 Winter Prose Poem Contest at *The Baltimore Review*: "Where My Mother Goes"

Shortlisted for the *2024 Bridport Poetry Prize:* "Ecstasy of Quiet Birds"